in her own words

k.d.lang

David Bennahum

OMNIBUS PRESS

LONDON / NEW YORK / PARIS / SYDNEY

Edited by Chris Charlesworth.
Cover & book designed by Michael Bell Design.
Picture research by David Brolan.

ISBN 0.7119.4307.9
Order No. OP47741

Exclusive Distributors:
Book Sales Limited
8/9 Frith Street, London W1V 5TZ, UK.

Music Sales Corporation
257 Park Avenue South, New York, NY 10010, USA.

Music Sales Pty Limited
120 Rothschild Avenue, Rosebery, NSW 2018, Australia.

To the Music Trade only:
Music Sales Limited
8/9 Frith Street, London W1V 5TZ, UK.

Photo credits:
Greg Allen/Retna: 4, 40, 45t, 76; John Atashian/Retna: 96b; A. J. Barrett/
Retna: 74; Fitzroy Barrett/Retna: 47l; Edie Baskin/Retna: 11, 75; Rob Brown/Retna: 23b;
Linda Chapman/Star File: 22; Dominick Conde/Star File: 88r, 94; Bill Davila/Retna: 46, 47r,
75, 88l, 96t; Steve Eichner/Retna: 87; Ken Friedman: 28b; Gary Gershoff/Retna: 91;
Harry Goodwin/Star File: 32br; Janey Gough/Celebrity Press: 48; Steve Granitnz/Retna: 84t;
Hames Hill/Retna: 70; Mick Hutson/Redferns: 13b, 85; Billy Jim/Retna: 68t;
Laurence Kirsch/Retna: 51t; Chris Kraft/Retna: 18l, 89; Andrea Laubach/Retna: 18r, 36;
Brett Lee/Star File: 78; Michael Linssen/Redferns: 84b, 92; Michael Llewellyn/Retna: 68b;
London Features International: 13t, 16, 17b, 20, 24, 25, 26t&b, 27t&b, 29, 32t, 41, 42,
49, 51b, 52, 55, 56, 57, 59, 63, 69, 79; Dorothy Low/Retna: 58; Henry McGee/Retna: 45b;
Marc Marnie/Redferns: 53, 86, 95; Joseph Marzullo/Retna: 33; Robert Matheu/Retna: 7;
Paul Natkin/Retna: 43; Barry Plummer: 50t; Valerie Phillips/Retna: 83; Chuck Pulin/
Star File: 10, 19, 28t, 30t, 37, 39, 44, 54, 62, 66; Redferns: 21, 23t, 34, 35, 93l&r;
David Redfern/Redferns: 30b, 60; Ebet Roberts/Redferns: 17t, 82; Ken Sharp/Q: 14, 71, 90;
John Spellman/Retna: 6, 8, 61; Star File: 12; Cleveland Starrs/Star File: 64; Nancy Thomas/
Star File: 31; Vinnie Zuffante/Star File: 32bl, 38, 50b, 72, 73, 80, 81.

A catalogue record for this book is available from the British Library.

About the author:
David Bennahum lives in New York. He writes for *The Economist*, *Wired*,
NetGuide, and is a contributing editor of *Lingua Franca* magazine. This is his third book.
He welcomes comments by email at davidsol@panix.com.

Printed in the United Kingdom by Scotprint Limited, Musselburgh, Edinburgh.

introduction

"I guess I just have a boring existence. People are doing biographies, but there's nothing interesting about me. I don't think they should do them until you're dead." k.d.lang, born Kathy Dawn Lang, on November 2, 1961, has had anything but a boring existence. From the time she fell in love with Anne Murray, Canada's country queen, Kathy Dawn knew she would become a star, and indeed she went on to earn greater fame than Murray ever achieved.

Raised in Consort, Alberta, a Canadian town with a population of 650 housed between oil fields and cow pastures, Kathy Dawn's life is the story of pure determination overwhelming a series of what to anyone else would be insurmountable barriers. Driven by the certainty that she would succeed, Kathy Dawn Lang changed her name to k.d.lang well before any success came her way. She created the image she wanted for herself based on her own terms and contradictions: androgynous yet attractive, mysterious yet accessible, eccentric yet serious, flippant yet emotional. She consciously chose to sing country because she thrives on being an outsider. The tension between her image and country's traditional conservative establishment fuelled some of her greatest achievements: recording with Patsy Cline's legendary producer after he'd gone into retirement, singing *Cryin'* with Roy Orbison, winning the Grammy Award in 1991 for Best Vocal Collaboration – yet through it all k.d. was paying a price.

Every time k.d. spoke out about something she believed in, she was attacked by the men who control country. A pantheist and firm believer in reincarnation, k.d. claimed she was the reincarnation of Patsy Cline. The many devout Christians that make up country's base found that insufferable. She stopped talking about Patsy and began taking a public stand on animal rights. Then ensued another, greater crisis. Its violence eventually drove k.d. out of country. She filmed an ad for PETA (People for the Ethical Treatment of Animals), asking the simple question: "We all love animals, but do we have to call some 'pets' and some 'dinner'?" The explosive reaction that followed broke her heart; it was terrifying, as she put it, to see the world turn against her. Country radio stations banned her music, fans returned albums, and the sign welcoming visitors to her home town was defaced to read: "Eat Beef Dyke".

In 1992, after a year in seclusion, k.d.'s life took an incredible turn for the better. She released *Ingénue*, her first album outside

of country, with great trepidation. The product of deep emotional revelation and the end of an intense love affair with a married woman, *Ingénue* marked the arrival of a new k.d.lang: vulnerable, tender and unabashedly authentic. *Ingénue* was a success beyond her expectations, selling eight million copies, and paving the way for her ground-breaking interview with *The Advocate* in which she publicly told the world she is a lesbian.

k.d., the pop star, went from eccentric anomaly to role model, becoming a symbol for acceptance and freedom. The warm embrace she received from many of her older fans, and the millions of new fans that followed her announcement, confirmed her greatest hope. She could be herself and still be loved. Today k.d.lang has not only redefined the public's acceptance of gay men and women, she also stands poised on the edge of a whole new beginning for her art, for her fans, and for herself. She's come a long way from the oil fields of Consort. But, partly in deference to k.d.'s disdain of biographies, don't let me tell you. Let k.d. speak, in her own words...

David Bennahum, September 1994.

growing up

roots

Alberta is a combination of Texas and Poland, oil wells and Slavics. I lived in Consort for 18 years. **1992**

We had a population of 650 people – and I think we had 650 eccentric people. In that size town, you know them intimately, so their eccentricities seem normal. I never thought to curb my own eccentricity. **1992**

(Consort had) one TV channel, one radio station, no movie theaters, one bar, one drugstore, no police – and no swimming pool. I guess when I was 10 we got a pavement. On one side was a slew, the other side was wheat fields. Lots of sky. Fields and sky. I was dying to get out, but I didn't hate it. I loved growing up there. I just knew that when it was time to leave I was going to leave. My dreams didn't have anything to do with staying there, but my roots are very happily situated there. **1993**

I think there's a certain freedom growing up in a limited cultural environment. It allows you to become more imaginative. If you're inundated with culture, sometimes you become jaded and start closing things off before you can assimilate them. **1993**

Growing up in Consort, you took what you could get, and you found something positive and creative in everything. Every sort of information I got would be a huge thing for my fantasy life. An album cover would be like a movie – a whole other dimension I would travel in, like stepping through the looking glass. Everything I ever did was part of the development of my imagination and lust for discovering new cultures and new sounds. **1993**

Growing up in a very culturally deprived environment can actually be a good thing because you edit your own snobbery. I would take in what I could get and I loved everything I got culturally. Although I think I do have a sense of taste, whether it's good or bad, I do see the positive aspect in almost all art. **1992**

I have this theory about small towns. The population is made up of eccentrics, everyone is eccentric. You know everyone and you know all of their idiosyncrasies; you just start to forget about 'em. That's how I take life.

It was exciting, (roller derby) was the only thing that came on TV on Saturday that was worth watching other than *The Beverly Hillbillies*. **1992**

In High School I took an aptitude test that said I was 98 percent guaranteed to be a mechanic. **1993**

I played absolutely every sport. **1992**

You know 650 unique people intimately. Eccentricity becomes normal. Everyone retains a uniqueness. Whereas in the city you tend to hang around people that you have things in common with. You don't get to know the guy on the street, whereas in a small town you know that guy. You know his history, you know his story, you know why he's there. And you know why the math teacher drives his tractor to school. **1992**

Bill Holmes drove his tractor to school every day. Eight o'clock, he'd drive his tractor past my house. **1992**

I'm really a small-town girl at heart. At the same time, I always wanted to be a musician and I was interested in cities. I was happy to be in Consort, but I wanted to get moving on. **1990**

You knew everyone from the day you were born till the day you could get yourself out of there. **1992**

There's been some turbulence between my roots and me, but what I loved about it I still love about it. I like the geography, the wind, the openness – not the people but the land. **1993**

I think there's something about a really severe (Canadian) winter that really calms people down. **1993**

family

My parents brought me up with no limitations. They supported my self-confidence and never said, "Only boys can do that." I rode motorcycles. I played sports. I did whatever I wanted to. But I'm probably a little cockier onstage than I am in real life. I have vulnerabilities and insecurities like anyone else. **1990**

I had really supportive parents. I remember my mother saying, "You're very handsome." I really loved that she said "handsome", because, you know, again, that's breaking stereotypes: you're very handsome, and you don't need to wear make-up. You have beautiful skin. **1992**

When I was nine, I wrote (Anne Murray) a song. I think it was called *Let's Try It Together*. It was a "we-are-the-world" type song. You have permission to write music to these lyrics, (I told her). **1992**

My father was a very charming man in public, and we liked him because he brought us stuff. **1993**

I was raised with no gender barriers and a real healthy dose of self-confidence. My father treated me like a tomboy. I did very "boy" things with him. He bought me a motorcycle when I was nine; I've been riding cycles for 22 years. I was a marksman; I used to shoot guns. But we shot targets; I never killed animals... I remember him getting me an electric guitar for Christmas when I was in grade six. **1993**

I love the wind. I love the feel of them. I love the aloneness. I love moving and seeing things. I like the romance of being on a motorcycle. **1993**

I was 170 pounds in the seventh grade, so I don't have a very healthy attitude towards my body. My brother and sister used to call me "Mama Kath Elliot", so I was scarred for life... but it has to do with more than siblings. It's social pressure, the pressure society puts on us to be beautiful, thin, stylish. **1993**

We were a pretty normal family. We had supper every night at six o'clock, and Saturday mornings I had to vacuum the carpet and clean the bathrooms. I loved both my parents very, very much, and of course I went into shock when my father left. **1993**

father

I don't think my father didn't love me. I just think he felt like he couldn't deal with what was happening in his own life. I knew there were troubles, but him leaving the way he did was a shock, and very hard to watch my mother go through. He left everything, so my mother would teach in the day and then go down and try to run the store. I had to take some of the responsibilities, whether it was working in the drugstore or getting home on time so my mother wouldn't worry. I went from being a kid to being an adult very fast. **1993**

k.d. in Sydney during a video shoot.

It was very sudden and drastic. I didn't hear from him for about eight years, until I ran into him on the street in Edmonton one

time. I haven't really talked to him since. I think I'm just processing it now. **1993**

I was really close to him before he left. Extremely close actually. And I ran into him a couple of times after about eight years. It just didn't seem necessary to work it up into some kind of forced relationship with him again. He didn't put any effort into it, so I just thought, well, I'll carry on. **1993**

I don't really feel angry at him. I guess my coping system is a *c'est la vie* attitude. A confidence, basically. Damage is one of the things in emotional aesthetics that makes something great, like all the scars on a tree or a banged-up coffee cup or whatever. Everything you go through is marking your soul. **1993**

childhood and music

Music played a huge part in my upbringing, and my family studied classical music every day. **1992**

My siblings and I studied classical piano for years. I sang in school, in competitions, around. **1990**

We also listened to Broadway shows. And I listened to Janis Joplin and The Allman Brothers. **1988**

I definitely practised in front of the full-length mirror. But not behind closed doors, god no. I wanted an audience all the time. **1990**

I just wanted to play guitar because it lent itself to accompanying singing the way I wanted to sing. I felt freer on the guitar. **1989**

k.d.'s first record:
It was an Anne Murray record. I think it was *What About Me?* I got it in the city somewhere. I was very young, but I was a huge fan of Anne Murray, the barefooted Canadian I saw on the television a bunch of times growing up.

I've listened to a lot of different music. Classical, my family's collection of Broadway material, Julie Andrews. **1990**

My first hero was Maria in *The Sound of Music*. I loved her wholesomeness and her happy-go-lucky attitude. I don't really know why I had such a rich fantasy life – maybe it's because I grew up in such culturally barren surroundings. **1992**

influences

performance art

I did things like crawling around on stage in garbage bags. I was in a 12 hour re-enactment of plastic heart surgery. **1987**

There was a breakthrough in heart surgery which we decided was pretty important, so we moved into an art gallery, set up an "operating theater" and mimed doing surgery for 12 hours. **1990**

I'm more focused on being a singer than a performance artist right now. **1989**

Performance art is all about seeing the different dimensions of a subject and conglomerating all your emotional responses without making a conclusive statement. For me, it was a natural step from that to country music. **1992**

wackiness

I am zany and crazy, but it has to be spontaneous. **1988**

The distance was expressed in k.d.'s glasses, the ones with no glass in them. They were a prop. But k.d. has become Kathy again; now there's no difference. I knew I was going to get trapped, with people expecting me to be strange and maybe not paying attention to the voice. Wearing a wedding dress is treacherous – every time I'm on TV they want zany and crazy k.d. lang. **1988**

I represent people who are a little bit quirky – people who always feel like they're getting stared at.

her name:
I like the way the small letters look. No special reason I did it, really. I liked e.e. cummings in high school. **1988**

I did it because Kathy's really mundane. k.d.'s generic and unlike Cherry Bomb, it is a name, not a sexuality. Then I started dressing up in the cut-off cowboy boots and the glasses. I played alternative clubs where they were favourable and then moved into the mainstream which was more difficult. In Alberta the cowboys are really straight; they don't like anybody fucking with their stuff. But somehow they liked me. I did lots of television and got really good press coverage. **1992**

I'm also alternative because of Canada – there's something romantic about being Canadian. We're a relatively unpopulated, somewhat civilized, and clean and resourceful country. I always push the fact that I'm Canadian. **1988**

When I go down to America it'll be totally different. They won't have seen what came before, so they won't think I've lost my edge. They're going to say: Look at this! **1987**

You can analyse me to death, but it's just that I grew up as a tomboy and I prefer my hair being short and I love Nudie suits.

There's a certain type of artist who isn't afraid to embrace mediocrity or kitsch and use it as an element. I think that really good artists aren't afraid to acknowledge the geek inside themselves. **1993**

To respect and to love something is also to understand the humour and absurdity in it. It is important to have fun with what you do. **1990**

I think I represent a lot of people who don't get represented a lot. I'm not a working girl's girl or anything, but I represent people who are a little bit quirky perhaps, people who always feel like they're getting stared at. What ultimately I would like to have happen is just to have people not feel any formularization pressure. I think that's what I stand for more than anything, the breaking of the mould. **1989**

As you can guess, I still receive a lot of resistance about the way I look. Particularly from the traditional country quarters. Still, I think it's loosened up a bit. Unfortunately, human beings evolve slowly. **1990**

That rockabilly rebel is still there, she's still inside, and it's like at the same time you're driving forward, you're waving good-bye, kinda unwillingly, at the beauty of being wacky and immature. **1993**

The wacky, crazy, kinetic k.d. lang began to override the music. My voice was playing second fiddle and I didn't want that to happen. **1987**

When I got rid of the glasses, things changed. That's when it came together. **1988**

You can't separate what's changing. When you change it's all encompassing. Obviously, cut-off cowboy boots and rockabilly outfits wouldn't fit this style of music. It doesn't fit my personality any more either. My appearance should reflect the changes I've undergone. **1992**

They think I've lost my edge, but I think the edge is just my short hair and the glasses and doing novelty songs. That's where I was then, and now that I'm taking my music more seriously and buying newer clothes, they're telling me I've lost my edge. Well, it's still there, it's just not as blatant as it was before.

It was my idea to do the barber thing. It was Herb's (Ritts) idea to get Cindy (Crawford), and it was a lot of fun. **1993**

I had such a reputation for being zany and crazy that I started to feel as if people wanted me to jump through flaming hoops all the time, when, ultimately I was a singer. I wanted people to focus on the music more than the novelty of my personality. **1992**

Right: On stage with Ben Mink at the Ritz in New York, June 1988.

I think being 'alternative', which most people think holds me back, actually helps. If I'd been an ordinary singer, I'd still be trying to get noticed in Canada. I'm alternative in every way. **1988**

music

I had a view of what I wanted to do when I was in the womb. It was never a question that I'd go into music but the only thing was what kind? **1992**

I loved it. I knew what I wanted to be the day I had my first piano lesson. I fell in love with music, and I'll stay in love forever. **1992**

It reflects what I'd listened to, as well as what, as a vocalist, I felt most moved by. I grew up listening to Broadway show stuff and classical. Now I'm listening to a lot of jazz singers, World Music, everything from Karen Carpenter to Kurt Weill. **1992**

Certainly I love to do my vocals live. There's just a different energy in the studio when you see the musicians actually playing it and it's actually going down on tape.

One of the reasons I coined the phrase (torch and twang) was to open things up for myself, so I wouldn't really want to define it. But the reasons I chose the words "torch and twang" is that I would love to marry ballad jazz and country. Those are the types of music I'm most passionate about. People have incorporated jazz into country before, but I don't think anyone's dedicated their life to it. **1990**

I detest borders in music. **1988**

Musically, I was only marginally interested in punk, but I loved its energy and rawness. **1992**

I listen to jazz more than anything right now. So I imagine it would have some kind of influence. I listen to the vocalists, some mainstream, bebop, some post-modern stuff. I listened to the pop station growing up in Consort, Alberta. I didn't listen to the country station. I wasn't fond of country music. **1990**

I like Thelonious a lot. Coltrane's my favourite, though. **1992**

Sometimes jazz drives me crazy, though. Especially people like Wynton Marsalis who are so fucking righteous. Wynton, loosen up will ya? They can be just as bad as the country people. **1992**

Maybe tons of people like (Karen Carpenter's) singing, but they kept it in the closet, because they think it's square to like her. But she was an amazing singer. I'm not saying she was progressive, but her pitch and tone and the richness of her voice were really incredible. I think the richness of her voice compares to Nat King Cole's. **1992**

That's the way they were marketed, (as syrupy-sweet). I try to overlook that, but not totally, because that was a part of it. I think you have to look at the positives and not worry what people will think of you for listening to The Carpenters. **1992**

I love easy listening. I find it a wonderful form of music for the kind of ballad singer I am. I know the term is used as a kind of insult, but you can't deny that Burt Bacharach is a great songwriter. Easy listening is just great songwriting by another name. **1992**

Rock'n'roll and soul are only slight influences for me. In pop music right now, they're just copying their ancestors. It's shallow. In soul music they're doing all these licks that are just condensed, saturated versions of what made the music great in the first place. **1992**

I like Dean Martin's singing a lot, and the fact he could make fun of himself... I am not afraid to say that I wouldn't mind being a lounge singer or a Vegas singer – one of those Dean Martins or Wayne Newtons – as long as in my head I felt hip. **1992**

I'm more and more influenced by classical music, Yma Sumac, Peggy Lee. As a singer, it was my inspiration to use the power of subtlety. Julie London was a big inspiration, Carmen McRae, all those singers who use their lower, softer register, more from an internal point of view. As a singer, that is a process of maturing. **1992**

Because my music is my lover and my child, I think that one of the reasons I changed at 30 to a softer kind of music was because I can't see myself jumping around the stage at 50. I don't want to. Of course I've never really been attracted to rock 'n' roll anyway... I find it really disturbing. It's a very male thing. **1992**

God bless Aretha Franklin...I do actually (think of writing R&B), but I don't want to talk about it. A kind of funk, yeah. Marvin Gaye-like. **1992**

Joni Mitchell is so advanced to me. And so deeply connected to the way I want to be. It's intimidating, and I have to just put her away. **1992**

There was a time when the voice and the lyric and the way you sang it was the ultimate thing. Now the most important thing is the rhythm. It's very dance oriented. Dance has always been important, but I dream of the day when crooners like Peggy Lee and Rosemary Clooney come back. **1990**

There's only one subject to ever talk about really. It's certainly the only thing to really write about...pain creates great art.

There's nothing like a good heartbreak to get a good song. **1992**

Of course I want to be in control, but control can be looked at as a negative thing these days – control freak. But control means being focused, in the driver's seat and persistent in the direction you want to go in. **1990**

I really just allow my instincts to take over when I'm making a new record. The main thing that applies to me in making music is that I've never done anything pure. **1992**

When I write I use a lot of sage because it's like getting stoned without having to smoke a joint. It kind of sets you into an alternative pattern. **1992**

It depends on whom I'm in love with. I think it's not important to be really specific. When I write, I don't even like to use "he" or "she". I always try to get away from that. I always use "I" or "they" or "you." **1992**

Another reason I don't use "he" and "she" is because I always try to write my love songs so that they can be applied to a dog or to God or to your mother. Love is not always the sexual level of love. **1992**

If I let everyone know everything, then it takes away the mystery of it. Even when I write a song, I don't want to be totally specific, because I want people to be able to interpret and apply it to their own situations. If somebody is too open and specific about what exactly their art means and is very analytical, it doesn't allow the listeners to take it and make it their own. **1992**

I have new ideas, but I'm sceptical about sharing them because every day they change. I might be in a more humorous mood, I might be in a more sexual mood; I won't know until I am there. I don't wait for inspiration; I go, okay, we have to get this record done – it's almost arbitrary. When artists have a successful record, there's a lot of unwritten pressure to formulate themselves. I'm pretty conscious of not doing that because I'm so spontaneous. **1992**

As an artist, vulnerability and innocence is something I strive for because I think that taps into the higher consciousness of art itself. **1992**

I try not to use my music as a vehicle. Interviews are the place for that. **1990**

country

patsy cline

I was acting in a local professional theater thing about country music called *Country Corral*. I was playing a role that basically emulated Patsy Cline, and my brothers and sisters said, "You should listen to her." Then people started telling me about her and giving me her records, and I saw *Coal Miner's Daughter*, and an influx of Patsy Cline material started pouring over me. **1988**

Before I played that part, I sort of knew who Patsy Cline was because of K-Tel ads on the TV. "Buy 24 Patsy Cline hits, blahblahblah..." That kind of thing. Then I got a whole bunch of her records and she really opened the doors for me to incorporate bebop and jazz and rock and rockabilly into country, which I had a very big love for. **1987**

She was the woman in country music. She was a sidestepper. She wasn't a victim, like Tammy Wynette. She was a strong woman, she really stepped out. **1987**

I think there's something to be said for being killed in your prime. You don't have to suffer like Elvis did. But it was still a tragedy that she died when she did. **1987**

Patsy Cline.

I think I am the reincarnation of Patsy Cline. You see, reincarnation is a very personal thing and it's as individual as people. But, I believe I have a very strong tie to Patsy because when I hear her music or I sing her music, I can absorb it so easily and so completely. I really don't want to talk about it, because in a community like Nashville, these people knew Patsy and then this kid from Canada comes down and it's like, "Big deal!" It's just such an honest thing, but it could be very detrimental if people don't understand.

Reincarnation is defined in the dictionary as "to continue to live", and I believe that Patsy Cline continues to live through me. Her energy, her spirit, whatever, I believe is part of me. I've started to feel reserved about talking about it, because there's been so much about it in the Canadian press. But it is a belief and it's a religion, almost. It's something that's so personal and so close that it's getting kinda difficult for me to discuss. **1987**

There's an energy I receive from her. When I was criticised for what I was saying about Patsy, I consulted her and I got my answer. **1988**

She was a very passionate and accomplished performer, and also she was a very strong woman working in a genre where women were expected to be passive. That hasn't changed at all, and I don't think it will. **1990**

If you took an ordinary person from my home town and gave them a great voice, that's Patsy. She was a very liberated, very progressive woman and a really soulful and honest singer. **1992**

Anyway, the whole thing's been done to death, pardon the pun. I'm not passing it off as a joke. What they can say is, "It's real, she believes it, but it's a personal thing, it's part of her religion, and she doesn't need to prove it. She doesn't want to be Shirley MacLaine."
1988

It was a method. There's a danger of sounding like it is almost disposable: you play the character, then it's over and you move on. It was much more spiritual for me. The fact that I worked with Owen was trying to fish in the stream of the whole Patsy Cline thing. I was real serious about Patsy Cline and was indebted to her for inspiring me to do the country thing, and truly touched, truly in love with the music. That's why I did k.d. lang and The Reclines for seven years – I was truly into it. **1992**

Patsy Cline.

Gram Parsons.

Emmylou Harris.

I felt very fortunate to get the chance to work with Owen and those musicians, and I realised that it was as close as I would get to Patsy on this earth. It's a difficult thing to talk about – it's rather like explaining how you feel about God. But, I did consciously try to let her influence come through. **1990**

She's kind of moved on. I think she checked out after *Shadowland*. I'm sure she's picked some young singer to pick on now. But she will always hold a real dear place in my heart. **1992**

country and western

I'm going to change country music. I mean, you've already seen it happen. Let's say Hank Williams was the first generation. Then you have people like Gram Parsons and Emmylou Harris. Then you have people like Rank and File and Jason and The Scorchers. And then you have people like Dwight Yoakam and k.d. lang. I am country music. I am a coalminer's daughter.

I don't think you have to overcome the fact that country isn't hip, because it is. It's all in the attitude.

(Country) deals with human emotions, and that's something I think we're all craving now.

I thought that country music was George Jones and Tammy Wynette. Period. In college, I started to open up. I came to country through Emmylou Harris and others – Anne Murray – among them – but Patsy Cline was the first real country artist I liked. I realized the music paralleled the environment I grew up in: I understand bake sales, the rodeo, the ordinary guy and girl. Hating the music at first, and then coming to it again, realizing how cool it is, gave me a kind of distance. **1988**

I didn't like country music until the late '70s. At that time I was doing sort of avant-garde folk, like The Roche Sisters or Jonathan Richman. I liked their sassiness, their humour, but yet dealing with very, very deep subjects. I came to country music through people like Emmylou Harris and Linda Ronstadt. They definitely opened the door for me. Definitely. **1989**

I came upon Patsy Cline when I was acting a role modelled after her in a professional country musical. I was 20. Although I had been toying with the idea of doing country, the direction and focus weren't clear until then. As soon as I heard her, the elements of my style, which I call "Torch and Twang," all came together. **1988**

I've always loved the music. But I take everything with a sense of humour. So yeah, I was doing it tongue-in-cheek, but I was also doing it respectfully. I really understand those values: I grew up in a town of 650 people, in Alberta, Canada. **1992**

Discovering that country was essentially white-North-American blues was a real turning point for me. It was very parallel to the way I grew up...it was sort of an acknowledgement of that lifestyle and environment. I was also drawn to country because we've entered a phase where music is very sterile and synthesized and narcissistic, while country music has a real humanistic quality to it.

Country still allows the singer and the song to have a good relationship. Pop music doesn't really allow that to happen right now, because the pendulum has swung so far into rhythm-oriented stuff. The country stuff was more about belting it out. **1992**

I grew up with country, but also saw the sense of humour in it, the kitschiness, and that attracted me to it. I also had been influenced by the punk scene, and I came from a performance-art background. Initially, the juxtaposition between performing art and country music totally turned me on. **1992**

When I first got to Nashville, I was given a pink handbook on how to be a country-and-western star. Section 1A, the first rule of country-and-western stardom, is, "The higher the hair, the closer to God." I tried, but it just wasn't me. **1990**

I don't eat meat and I'm not a Christian and I don't have big fluffy hair, which basically stands against a lot of the Americanisms and the fundamentalist values on which country music is based. But at the same time, I understand and appreciate all those values. I just see wide, or beyond those things. Like, I'm not opposed to Christianity, but I see that Buddhism and Hare Krishna have a place too.

It's closed to cultural differences. **1990**

There's things about country music I still don't like, the limited theme of country lyrics generally. I think country music is still very prejudiced in gender, in race, in religion, and I think that needs to be widened. One of the things that intrigued me about country music was the potential to broaden the lyrics and consciousness. There's been a misconception that country listeners don't want to be challenged, and I think that's wrong. I think they do as much as anybody else. Although we deal with really basic humanistic and emotional subjects, you can do that on different levels. **1989**

I value what I learned (from performance art), but it was so limitless that there were no boundaries to work within and try to change. That's why I chose country music. It has such a structure that I find the potential to challenge it really exciting.

My starting in country music was a combination of being at the age when you start to appreciate your roots and frustration with the constant struggle to be bizarre and over the top with performance art. I was really really ready to hit the scene. It was total, unbridled kinetic verve. I didn't have a lot of artist friends growing up. I was a jock, basically; that's what kept me going. And I was exploding being around other people, other artists, people who were feeding me and also taking from me. I had an audience. **1993**

I think I challenged them at the beginning. But I think just a matter of time and hearing me sing and hearing me talk about my sincerity and integrity towards country music, that they really start to appreciate and accept me. I don't think I'm a good old boy, but I think I value what they stand for. The thing about me is that I would like to bring the country audiences a little closer to the middle and the people on the left a little closer to the middle, too, and people who are too artsy to like country and people who are too country to like art.

Somewhere along the way (country) got too sophisticated and embarrassed about people who were "too country." It was way overdue to have an androgynous singer. **1988**

I'm certainly not singing about the Marlboro man when I'm up there! **1992**

The fans of country music in Europe are more romantic about it, because they don't have to live with all the rednecks who are involved with it over here. **1990**

One thing I'd like to do is introduce other religions to country music, which is so dominated by Christianity. **1988**

One of the things that enticed me was the challenge of country music – to change it a little bit. It's not that I want to change it exactly, but I think there's a certain void in country that I'd like to fill.

I don't think I overcame the fact that country isn't hip, because it is – it's very hip! It's all in the attitude and I think there are extremes: it's either very hip or very corny.

Country mixed my reality and my fantasy together because my fantasy was to be a star. I'd always looked on it as a less intelligent form of music like hip people do, but then I really started to love it. I liked the kitsch aspect but I also like the value system of it. It's like a mixture of blues and Christian values, and it's very extreme. Performance art got a bit boring because there were no barriers to fight against. One of the things I found most interesting about country was the idea of being creative inside a structure. **1992**

The country industry is traditional regarding the looks and roles of men and women. I've been made to feel that if I played by their rules and expectations, I'd sell more records. It would be detrimental for me to compromise. I sing because of the way I am. I don't want to endanger my soul and my voice because of my physical looks. It wouldn't be worth it. **1990**

Nashville is an ugly little city. They hate the Blacks and there's no one there but white Christians and Blacks. **1990**

It's kind of a weird paradox. I'm accepted artistically in Nashville. I performed on the CMA Awards, but I'm not nominated for any. Country is intimidated by me or scared. **1989**

My life is split in two – the alternative scene and the country scene. I haven't experienced any prejudice in the alternative scene, except maybe to my music because it's "too country." But the prejudice I feel from radio programmers in the country market is about my image. **1990**

At one time there were a lot of people like Steve Earle, Lyle Lovett, Dwight Yoakam and so on who were making waves; but what's happened is that some of those people became more traditional, and others got pushed out until they gave up. **1990**

Even though I was never accepted on country radio and I was never embraced by the Nashville political establishment, I could play the Grand Ole Opry once and I could be a part of their big outdoor festivals because I drew people and I could be on their TV shows because I was good viewing. I brought new viewers. But they never wanted to embrace me. And I understand why. I didn't want to ever be embraced. **1992**

k.d. with Lyle Lovett.

k.d. with Dwight Yoakam.

Roy Orbison.

roy orbison

They wanted it to be a duet and I said it should be either Roy (Orbison) singing or me singing. It shouldn't be a duet. I started to wake up and go, "It's Roy Orbison that you'll be singing with, you goon." **1992**

I wouldn't have considered doing a duet of *Cryin'* with a girl until I heard her sing. **1988**
Roy Orbison

I wanted to do really well for Roy. **1989**

His involvement in my life, however short, was so multifaceted and so golden I'm still feeling the benefits of it. **1992**

His strength and his calmness and his unworldly faith will affect me forever. He was so beyond the surface and the frivolous part of human nature. I mean, people always thought he was so lonely and sad and everything, but *au contraire*, he was very strong and very peaceful. He was a legend and yet he was really humble. **1992**

To have the right head and sing a standard like (*Cryin'*) is a wonderful thing. I always think of Roy when I sing it... peaceful and quiet like a tree. His cheek was softer than mine. **1992**

k.d. with Andy Bell of Erasure.

collaboration

I don't want all of a sudden to be duets with a whole lot
of people because in some ways it would take away from the
greatness of the Roy thing. It's not because I'm real snobby.
So now Willie Nelson is singing with Sinéad O'Connor. Well there's
been so much it doesn't become a special union. **1990**

Personality and communication are just an extension of art.
For example, Joni Mitchell: she was talking about painting and
I was so intimidated that I was going to say something stupid that
I couldn't talk. It was almost the same with Dylan; he was talking
about songwriting, and I didn't want to say something stupid.
He was saying he wanted to write with me, and I really don't know
if that was... sometimes these things are just something to say.
I think the same thing about writing with people as I do about
singing with people. Even though I think that Bob Dylan is a
tremendous song writer, it would be really hard to work with
someone like him. It's like taking two distinct ingredients and
putting them together, like curry and chocolate. **1990**

Greatness doesn't intimidate. Idiots intimidate. Working with great
people, you feel honoured, humbled and blessed. **1988**

writing with ben mink

It's like walking down a long, dark, corridor, myopically focused
on what I'm doing, yet seeing glimpses, audio-glimpses, of what
I want to do musically, groove-wise or with instrumentation and
how I want to project my voice. My internal banks either store it or
edit it out. I never use a tape machine. Ben is completely the
opposite; he's constantly recording and mixing stuff, playing guitar
and cataloguing it on tape. I'm not a technical person at all. I work
from instinct, a very primal arena. That's why I value Ben so
much; he manages to capture the little ideas. I don't want to
spoil that. **1990**

When Ben and I write, we try to strip ourselves of what we have
learned and write from a real primal and innocent place. We apply
our knowledge at a later point. But at the initial stage of
conception, we try to do it very raw. **1992**

We share a vision of what we can do in country music. I'm the
one who starts with titles and ideas. But when we actually get
down to writing, he starts with a riff, a drum pattern, with a fell.
Then we get together and sort out what's good.

When I'm off writing the lyrics and melody, he's putting down the form on tape and arranging the tune. So the actual process from conception to the finish is about four days. Which is really fast. **1990**

I've often caught myself feeling a little scared if he should leave me. But I was a songwriter before I met him and I write songs on my own occasionally...but why worry about it? As far as I know, we're writing the next record together. **1990**

k.d. with Greg Penny (left) and Ben Mink (right) at the Canadian Juno Awards.

leaving country

I love country music. But the feeling from the Nashville community wasn't entirely mutual. It's a real funny market. The pendulum has swung back to traditionalism and there's no place for someone like me. There have always been these outlaws, left-of-centre country artists like Rank and File and before that Rosanne Cash and before that Johnny Cash and Waylon (Jennings) and Willie (Nelson). **1992**

If I kept on doing something I didn't feel like doing, it would have been creative suicide. **1992**

The Reclines had developed a certain sound, it was a country sound and I just wanted to change. **1992**

I certainly am a person who lives by the rule that change is the essence of growth. Change is what fuels me. So I felt it was time

for me to move on from country. I mean, I had won the Grammy,
but still wasn't getting airplay, and I had been as creative as
possible with country music... It's like a lover that it's time to leave.
1992

Country music was something that courted me, and totally
stole my passion for seven or eight years. But now the earliest
influences – Broadway, film and classical music – are shifting
again to the top. And with this surfacing comes the real
emancipation of my vocals, and my passion as a vocalist. I think
that there's not a lot of vehicles for a vocalist of my nature. It's
about making my own market and giving myself somewhere to be
as a singer. **1992**

I think I've always been really honest about the fact that
country music was a period of my life, and that I'm interested
and influenced by so many more things. I think you witnessed a
woman who was 21 and just sort of burst into art and was frantic
about it. I don't really know about the process of me maturing,
or my art maturing. You've seen me for 10 years already, believe
it or not. It's just me growing up in public. **1992**

I was just following my basic instincts, my desires and needs as
an artist. Through my whole career I made it clear that music was
my fundamental love and it didn't matter about the genre. So it
was really about letting go of one lover and embracing another.
As for country music, the passion had just died. Rather than
struggle, I decided to follow my calling. **1992**

I think the time has come for me to let go of the idea of being a
country singer. Country will always be a major influence on me,
but I've also been influenced by everything from opera to Ofra
Haza; and I'm not prepared to make the kind of compromises that
would be necessary for me to be accepted by these people.
At one time I did very much want to prove to them how much
I honestly loved country music, but they make their assessments
whether you're honest or not. **1990**

I don't want to be bitter about the country music scene. I did it
with respect and with humour. But it's like a love affair. It's over.
It's time to move on. **1992**

I still love early country music. There was always an adversity
in my relationship with the political establishment of country, and
I think that's what kept me challenged, but to be bitter about it
would be wrong. What made me change was that I wanted to
explore the different personalities within my music. **1992**

You know, it's basically a very conservative, male, Christian, conformist kind of place. I was different. And Nashville is not a place where difference is appreciated. Also, I did it for quite a while and musically I needed a new challenge. **1992**

I always knew I could never limit myself to one specific area of music, and this was a natural point in my life to change the style. I loved the form, the gut-level emotion and honesty of country; those combined with the stereotypical lyrics and attitudes appealed to me. The contradiction of playing the really strong female within what is basically a submissive role, I found extremely exciting. **1992**

I moved away from country because I've always planned to have a career that involved a lot of change and it was just time. Having to stick to one style was starting to make me burst at the seams. **1992**

I never professed to be a country artist. I just think that country music has influenced me. I was honest about my influences and about this probable need to change them from the very beginning. **1992**

I think the fans will come with me because I'd like to think it's sort of like Roy Orbison or Ray Charles – the people who can be just singers, you know? You can have country fans and also just be a singer, and that actually is what appeals most to me, just being known as a singer and not one specific genre.

I would prefer to build an audience slowly and one that is not necessarily a country audience. **1988**

I'd like to sell to the people like me who looked at country music the same way I did. This music was a very important part of me and I think it can be for a lot of other people too.

I don't think I can wipe the slate clean. Country music is very melodic and lyric based; it's very much about the singer and the song. There's an honesty and passion to country music that really appeals to me, and I hope that's still a part of my music. **1992**

I always knew I was an alternative artist, and I try to explain it as Nashville and I were mutually user-friendly. I wanted to be on the periphery of the country mainstream and not in it, though it always looked like I was fighting in it. I would have hated to have become Reba McEntire; there would have been too many compromises to get there. **1992**

They loved the fact I brought new viewers but didn't want to accept or subscribe to my viewpoints – vegetarianism, lesbianism, things that definitely don't suit the stereotypical role of the female. I raised issues and they didn't want to be responsible for putting someone like myself on the radio who was against the values of the listeners. **1992**

I think it was a mutual parting. I don't feel any bitterness toward the industry at all... I think I retained an alternative edge. I think they enjoyed my quirkiness, but at the same time they didn't want to take responsibility for my actions or my being. **1992**

I'm not bitter or above it but I think a lot of it was watered down. They were always afraid to let the humour and hillbilliness shine through. And maybe the country isn't there any more. In the backwoods of Kentucky there are satellite dishes. It's all urbanized. **1992**

Country music was a part of my life. Now it isn't. We had a good relationship, really, but we wanted each other at arm's length. The people in Nashville didn't want to be responsible for my looks or my actions. But they sure did like the listeners I brought. **1992**

I loved being as successful as I was and yet retaining sort of this outlaw image. I think in some way the community will be relieved, because they won't have to deal with me any more – I'm talking specifically of the business aspect. **1992**

Looking back it was perfect. I had success, like the Grammy for Best Female Vocalist, and yet never had airplay and never a CMA (Country Music Association) nomination, so you had this huge contradiction, which is what I thrive on. **1992**

My country career was exactly what I wanted. I was successful enough and yet always maintained a sort of alternative image, an edge. I was upset that I didn't get airplay, but now I think that was exactly what I always wanted. **1992**

They didn't want someone who looked like me, who thought like me, who spoke out like me. They wanted to take the value of me involved in their system. And that's fair because I did the same. I used them too. **1992**

beliefs

vegetarianism & health

It was always in me. But it would have been a little tough to grow up where I did and say, "Mom, don't cook animals."

I'm an almost militant vegetarian, an animal rights activist. Even my dog's a vegetarian. Eats couscous, soy protein, garlic and broccoli. I'd bring her with me on the road – it'd be like a piece of God running around – but it would be too hard on her. **1990**

I'm a country singer who's a vegetarian for health reasons and because of compassion for animals. **1988**

Cruelty to animals was my biggest beef with make-up. **1992**

I'm old fashioned about lying, stealing and cheating. But even with my strong beliefs that are not old fashioned – about vegetarianism for instance – I try to be open to other people. When I go out to Consort with my cowboy friends from childhood and round up cattle, I lecture them a little on vegetarianism, but at the same time, I can't lecture. I believe the strongest example in anything is a silent example. **1988**

I haven't had a drink in a year. I don't smoke. I'm a vegetarian. I drink about a litre of Evian a day – very Californian. I look funny in make-up. I only wear it when it's impossible for me to get out of it. I wouldn't armwrestle a photographer over a little base.

spirituality

I was 24 before I even knew what a bagel was. But I loved Jewish culture, and my friends made me an honorary Jew. I am a real Jew. I was raised a Christian for the first 13 years. Who knew? I liked those corny things like God and you walking down the sand and you go, wait a minute, there's only one set of footprints, and it's God. And then I went through an atheist stage. I think it's called adolescence. **1993**

I'm a very strong moral person, I'm really straight in that sense, but in terms of religion, I'm really open. **1988**

I'm honest and sincere, which is a pretty heavy label to pin on yourself. I try to take myself lightly. I mean I take my singing seriously, but otherwise I just look for the humour in everything and try to stay open to whatever happens.

I enjoy the wisdom and maturity that comes with age. I think I'm more subtle, more emotional, softer. I've relinquished the control I thought I had. By being less in charge, I'm more in charge. I've found comfort in the realization that you're really not in control ever. **1992**

The yin and the yang of it is that life should have cynicism and humour, as well as respect and integrity. That's my basic approach to everything – including my art and music. **1989**

Maybe I've developed my spirituality around coping, but I truly believe it's the law of nature that love isn't something we necessarily own. It isn't necessarily shared. There are moments of sharing, but I don't think there are any rules. **1993**

I read three things: graffiti, the phone book, and the dictionary. If you spend two hours reading your book, I'll spend two hours reading the way a bug will crawl up a leaf. I really spend more time in nature than anywhere else. I learn from nature. **1992**

I just don't have the concentration for anything else. One word or a sentence, and I'm off. I'll read it, and my mind is all over the world. **1992**

I write some other things that aren't songs – poetry, short stories or whatever. But, to be quite honest, I do not read. **1989**

I guess nature is really my starting point, my ground zero. It's from being from the country, I guess. Even today, when I'm pondering some stupid human question, I watch nature. Because it seems so pure, even though it's cruel. That's part of it. It's just sort of comforting for me. **1993**

I'm sort of a pantheist; I see God in everything, whether it's a pair of running shoes or a whale. **1993**

I believe that all things are connected. **1992**

I'm into past-life regression and everything. **1992**

I have thousands of philosophies, but none that can be (described) in a paragraph or less. At one point I felt very strongly about letting people know about my (personal beliefs), but North Americans aren't really that open-minded when it comes to things like reincarnation. **1988**

People who hate (make me angry). Like really fundamentalist Christians. And people who judge drive me crazy. I hate people who judge, I think we all judge, but I mean people who actively and hatefully judge. **1992**

You see, people say Jesus died for them, but that cow died for you, and all people do is go into Safeway and bitch about the price... Not everyone believes in Christ. Or should. I'm not opposed to Christ, but I think there are problems in North America that stem from the idea you have to fear God. **1988**

The fact that anyone could say that AIDS is God's way of paying back homosexuals is really disturbing. If that's true, then lesbians are angels. **1992**

I'm very into omens. A lot of decisions are made by flipping a coin. And I don't fuck with it. When I flip a coin, that's the way it is. The coin doesn't lie. **1990**

If I see a crow somewhere where a crow wouldn't usually be, it's some sort of a sign. I consider myself a crow. I don't know why. I just feel I have an affiliation towards them. **1990**

I watch crows. They sort of teach me how to dance – that sounds so corny sometimes, I can't stand it. But it really is true.

I do contradict myself. My philosophies and my ideals are constantly changing, and I think that's healthy. I think that whatever I do, I believe at that moment. I try not to do anything that doesn't represent me properly. **1992**

Whatever you do has to stem from your absolute beliefs. If I really tried to mould myself into what was politically correct and actually didn't feel it, then it would just be a mess. Ultimately my artistry dominates anything I do, and that encompasses the transcending of any sort of gender categorization in my music. I want the listener to apply what I say to their own individual situation, whether it applies to your dog, God, your mother, your lover – whatever. **1992**

k.d. with fellow anti-fur trade protesters at the Hard Rock Café in New York.

PETA

Text of the never-aired PETA advertisement:
We all love animals, but why do we call some "pets" and some "dinner"? If you knew how meat was made, you'd probably lose your lunch. I know – I'm from cattle country, and that's why I became a vegetarian. Meat stinks, and not just for animals, but for human health and the environment.

It caused a big stink when I was promoting vegetarianism and said, "meat stinks," which was meant to be a touch of comic relief. I don't believe that killing animals for culinary needs is necessary or right. **1992**

Seeing the way farm animals were treated up close made it easier to be against it. **1990**

How can you place human life above every other form of life. Who do these people think they are? **1992**

The music establishment as well as cattlemen felt that I had betrayed them by speaking out. It's basic human nature to look for something to hate in somebody, especially somebody slightly controversial. They're just waiting for you to do something wrong. It hurt me a lot, not in a business sense or a public sense, but it made my mother and my family suffer, and that was hard. **1992**

It hurt my mom. And nothing is really worth that. **1992**

The vortex of the controversy was in my home town. It wasn't so much the criticism of the press. It was the personal attacks on my family that were really painful. Alberta is a small place. Everyone treats you like you're their own. They're your best fans but they're also your worst critics. It can be very double-sided. **1992**

There's the thing like, "Oh, k.d.'s become famous." And soon they have something to hate me for, like the beef thing, they say, "I knew it. I knew it. She's...she's not right." **1992**

They sprayed EAT BEEF DYKE on it. *The Consort town sign.* **1993**

In Alberta, I think they felt I'm theirs and I betrayed them.
There were letters and lots of negative commentary in the local
paper, and people called up the radio station saying don't play her
records. In that community, meat is how they make their dollar,
that's been their lifestyle, and I can understand how the "Meat
Stinks" campaign is threatening. Now, I love those people –
they're ingrained in my soul and my past – but I can't see that
eating meat is ultimately a good thing. **1992**

I went from being Canada's little queen to all of a sudden having
the whole country against me. It's a little scary to feel that wave
shift. **1992**

The funny thing was that when I made the "Meat Stinks"
statement, they said they banned my records. Well, the truth was
that no one was playing my records anyway. **1992**

Warner (Records) thrived on the publicity. At first they thought
it might hurt sales. But those men in the trucks out there, those
aren't the guys you see at my concerts. **1992**

Radio stations that never played me in the first place were
banning me. I didn't care so much that they weren't playing my
records. **1992**

And you know the beef commission. As soon as they get this,
they're gonna say "Lesbians don't eat meat." **1992**

I wasn't prepared for the response, no. But, looking back now,
I don't think it was [a mistake]. It's obviously an extension of my
beliefs; it's an extension of my personality. And the reaction was
an extension of society. So it's exemplary of what's really
happening. It was painful and very stressful, but my stance on the
issue remains even stronger. So, no, I don't think it was a mistake.
1992

k.d. with Liza Minnelli.

business

making it

first job:
I auditioned and got the job. The band folded, but by then I had met my manager, who owned the studio we rehearsed in. I kept in touch with him, and about eight months later I went back and said, "I'm ready to record a single." And he said, "I'd like to manage you." So we started. I put a band together, did a gig, got some press, then moved to Toronto and got national press. Then I made a record, got more press, and signed with Sire Records. **1988**

I'm a bit nervous about The Bottom Line. There's going to be lots of record people there... I really don't know what to expect. **1985**

I was playing at the Bottom Line (in New York) and I'd been talking to a bunch of record companies. Then Seymour Stein, the head of Sire, came backstage and asked "Do you know *Ballad of a Teenage Queen* by Johnny Cash and *She's No Angel* by Kitty Wells?" I just looked at him because, of course – Madonna, Talking Heads, and The Pretenders – he's signed all of 'em and those names pretty much speak for themselves as far as artists go. And here he is knowing all about country music and who played on which records. I just looked at him and it was love at first sight.

selling music

I listen to the people that I trust at the record company, and I think of them as artists at what they do. **1992**

These people have known me for eight years. They know what I would approve of and what I wouldn't and I trust them. **1992**

I love my record company. I'm sure I'm one of the few artists that can say that. **1992**

Some days I feel like I'm doing nothing but paying dues, and some days I think there are no dues at all. As corny as it sounds, I just thank God that I do what I do. I'm glad I don't work in an office building. Not that that's wrong, but it would be wrong for me. Actually there are certain things that come to mind as kind of scary challenges – like opening for Hank Williams, Jr., in the

Seymour Stein, who signed k.d. to his Sire Records label.

Midwest. But, in retrospect, I did it and I survived, so it becomes an elaboration, not another due. All these things, looking back, enhance your history. **1992**

I don't want to sell my music through sexuality. **1992**

I do use (sexuality) onstage. It's a really hard thing to talk about. I don't want to be out like Phranc is out. **1992**

record industry men:

I think I intimidate them. I'm not speaking self-righteously, but I think that if I am hassled by men they don't do it to my face. They do it, you know, politically. **1990**

I don't do things that I can't justify to myself. Men aren't used to a woman responding aggressively the way I do. We all know that an aggressive woman is considered a bitch but aggression in a man is a good business trait. **1990**

There's just a disappointing circumstance of the availability of women musicians... I think it's because it's not encouraged at an early age, because there's not a lot of role models on MTV who are playing drums, who are playing guitars. And at a certain point it may be an age thing too. I heard Annie Lennox the other day talking about this new era of senior rock-and-rollism: The Rolling Stones, The Who... but where are the women? Maybe Tina Turner. **1992**

It costs me a lot to tour. Eight band members, 22 in my crew, two buses, a truck. **1990**

It's hard to second guess radio. I could grow my hair, wear pretty little dresses and then go around to all the country stations. Gimmicks don't make it with me... I have a solid base of fans and my popularity is growing. But if you want to buy a house, you need to be on the radio. **1989**

Well, I haven't got any money yet. You know how long it takes. And if you don't get radio play... that's really where the money is. **1990**

I won a Grammy for best country artist. But I still wasn't played on country radio. I finally stopped and asked myself how much further I wanted to push this thing. **1992**

Darlene, my assistant, makes my life a lot easier. Does just about everything, darns my socks. I guess she's sort of a wife. **1990**

I think I've been successful. I play sold-out audiences and I play music on uncompromising terms. I think that's as successful as one can ask for. In terms of formulated success, having hit singles and selling lots of records, that's not where I'm successful. **1990**

The music business is so damned unpredictable. Either I'll be so rich I can't get arrested, or I'll be rich and can't get a job. Or I'll still be plugging away. Or I'll be dead. **1990**

awards

I promise to deserve this award. I promise to work hard next year. I promise to always sing for the right reasons.
Acceptance speech, Juno Award, 1985

I thought it was most appropriate (coming in a wedding dress). But lots of people didn't get it. **1988**
Juno Award

I felt a little bit like a rebel, unaccepted. Knowing they are behind me, after all, has certainly given me and the band a boost. **1988**
Canadian Music Association Award

My award was a major subject of controversy. A lot of country people got really upset about it. But I didn't. That was a big award for me. It proved I was making progress. I felt motivated, excited, relieved...yeah, because it was over.
Grammy Best Vocal Collaboration Prize 1988

records & films

angel with a lariat

I just wanted to make an album: I was itching to get down and get some exposure in the States. **1988**

I like that record now, but I hated it for years. Tons and tons and tons of reverb, 150 milliseconds on everything. **1993**

Financially it was really stupid. They really wanted (Dave) Edmunds and I just really wanted to record the album. I think one of the best things about it was we were all on edge. Just the idea of being someplace new. London's a real music city, it has lots of history, and the edge of that came out in the studio.

We had just a month and I'm not sure Dave wanted to do it. I was over-emotional because I was 23 and wanted to be a star... between my music and my image (*Angel With A Lariat*) was just too much for country radio. **1992**

It was so stressful. Part of it was that he didn't understand what I was doing and I was so hyper and enthusiastic and overly emotional. I just wanted to get my record out and I wanted to be a big star right away. **1992**

It's an interesting album, and I don't regret it. But my vocal wasn't pushed nearly as much as it should have been. What I'm trying to do is hard for anyone to understand, let alone – with all due respect – an Englishman. I think he didn't really understand the sincerity with which I approach country music. The English view is a very romantic thing. I don't think they understand the love hate relationship many of us have with it. **1988**

If someone could convince me that Dave Edmunds' strategy
was to get me wound up so I'd get involved in my album, then
I'd say he was a great producer. But I'm not convinced that was
his strategy.

I've started to like it again. It's kind of peppy. **1992**

shadowland

Shadowland came out at an odd time in my career in that it is only
my second album. It wasn't strategically planned. I simply had the
opportunity to work with one of my idols and I took it. That's what
was so special about the record. It was a gift. **1988**

This is the sound that motivated me to dedicate myself to country
music. Being a major Patsy Cline fan and listening to Loretta
(Lynn), Kitty (Wells) and Brenda (Lee), I realized that they shared
the common denominator of having worked with Owen (Bradley).

It was a magical session, the end of a dream, the end of the
rainbow. Politically, this album is very correct. I mean, working
with Nashville session players, in Nashville, with Nashville's most
celebrated producer. It's going to be very interesting to see how
they swallow the next Reclines record. I've gotten the first taste
of acceptance, but the game's not over.

Shadowland and (producer) Owen Bradley are very, very important
to me. I may record with Owen again, sometime down the road,
but right now I'm looking at it as a one-time special thing.

Shadowland was the purest I got, and that was because it was
done as a retrospective album. My own songwriting and producing
is always a balance between progressive and retrospective, but it's
a very fine balance. **1992**

The biggest thing I learned was to be able to sing songs
that I wouldn't necessarily have recorded in my career with
The Reclines. Songs like *Sugar Moon*, very light, very digestible,
one-dimensional songs.

I wanted to use The Reclines, but (Bradley) didn't want to have
to deal with learning the communication system between five new
musicians. I think The Reclines were put off at first but I think they
realize now it was an opportunity I had to fulfill.

(Bradley) did so much to shape (Patsy Cline's) sound in the studio. He's one of the best country producers in terms of incubating the vocals. He's really into straight ahead lyrics and subject matter everyone can understand. It's almost a totally different school from where I come from.

Through my love for Patsy Cline, I sought after Owen, who produced every record she ever made, along with Loretta Lynn, Red Foley, Ernest Tubb and Brenda Lee. Finally he said yeah. It was magical. **1992**

Brenda (Lee) is a very technical singer, Kitty (Wells) is so serene and maternal, and Loretta (Lynn) is exactly what you thought she would be like. She came into the studio with a pound of bologna and a loaf of white bread so everyone had bologna sandwiches. I almost ate one! I'm a vegetarian but I thought it was blessed food.

They have a persona they developed in their prime. I am a woman of the late 1980s and have been influenced by punk and by Boy George. **1988**

These are the people who have most influenced me. It was like working with the teachers. **1988**

They of course were three of the big four women Owen produced. I took the place of Patsy, who was the other one. **1988**

I played him *Pine and Stew* and he called it a "novelty." I don't think he understands the way young artists can mock and respect at the same time. It goes back to what I said about straight ahead lyrics. His thing about country music is that you understand every lyric and the emotions you are trying to put across.

(Bradley) is very attentive, accommodating and jovial. He doesn't say too much to the band or the singer until there's a dead end or a problem. He sits back a lot and listens but he keeps the mood of the session very high. If I felt there was a problem he was very open to my suggestions. Anything to make a vocal more comfortable he would do.

Once we selected the material we'd practise. Just (Bradley) on piano and me singing. We'd only practise a song two or three times a day, and the rest of the day, which would be about five hours, we would spend listening to great jazz vocalists like Carmen McRae, Ella, and Peggy Lee. We'd also listen to hillbilly singers and saxophonists like Jimmy Hodges, Ben Webster, people like that. What we really did was start a communication system on what we liked and what we thought was weak about vocal styles.

On the first sessions, we were focusing on songs we both had wanted to do for a long time... we did a song he did with his big band a long time ago called *Shadow Land*. It's a real jazz song and definitely not commercial in any way, but it really pulled something from both of us that we wanted to accomplish. It was sort of like country jazz. **1988**

Working with Owen and having achieved that kind of music, I feel relieved knowing I've done it. I'd love to see it become famous and considered a historical thing, of course, but the main thing is, I did it. I've worked with the master of the kind of music I've studied, and heard him say, "You're as good as Patsy Cline." **1988**

absolute torch and twang

It represents the maturing process of k.d. lang and The Reclines. **1989**

(*Wallflower Waltz*) celebrates physical bigness and internal bigness. It's about artists and the people who made a conscious decision to become observers rather than participants in the social structure. **1989**

We look at those billboard kings and queens and think, "Oh, he's so beautiful, she's so beautiful, I want to be like them." I don't think that's healthy. I've written a song called *Wallflower Waltz*. It's about accepting yourself and not striving to be an image invented by other people. **1988**

It was written as a reaction to a friend's story. Every song stems from a personal experience, don't you think? It wasn't necessarily written about myself. As I said, my personal thing is animals. Women's rights of course, but my number one protectionist energy goes towards animals maybe even before women. If people could respect animals, they might respect themselves more. **1990**

ingénue

Ingénue is based on my experiences of falling in love, and it's the most personally revealing record I've ever made. The writing is totally autobiographical, naked and real – if I was toothpaste and you squeezed me, you'd get *Ingénue*. **1992**

During this time I fell in love for the first time and it's an overwhelming experience. The theme of the record is obviously love but it's getting to a point of love where you realize you have no control and you can't manipulate it. And that love is about pain as well as pleasure. It's about relinquishing control to love. I experienced a period where I thought, "Wow, I'm not going to conquer the world like I thought I was going to. I don't have it on a string. It's a period of great awakening and realizing that this is the way you are and you have to live with it. **1992**

I look at *Ingénue* as a type of non-harmful dope. That's the way we expected it to be, and that's the way we created it – a hypnotic kind of trip. **1992**

(*Ingénue*) means unworldly, naïve, artless. An unworldly artless woman played by an actress. **1992**

This isn't a country record. This was complete emancipation for me. I wrote it for myself. **1992**

This album is emotional puberty for me. The songs focus on unrequited love... the worst kind. But I think that it has a positive overtone. **1992**

Now I know people like me, I can be less theatrical. I don't need to hide behind façades. *Ingénue* was the result of me going from 28 to 30. It's called the Saturn return and I've heard that a lot of women go through it... I don't know, I'm just glad I'm on the other side of it. **1992**

There's not too many romantics out there right now. I think every album I ever did I thought was being vulnerable and honest, but certainly I think *Ingénue* is my most vulnerable and honest work. I hope I haven't peaked in that area, but I think part of that is maturing as a person, as a woman. **1992**

It's just that in your 20s, it's like going to the buffet in a new restaurant. After you try everything a few times, you narrow it down to the couple of things you really like. And if it was a type of guard, it was a completely natural thing, like the quills on a porcupine. I mean, when people say, "Oh, *Ingénue* is so much more vulnerable, so much more honest," it's just that I'm more pathetic now. **1993**

Whether it was lyrically or musically or personality wise or fashion wise, it's all an extension of the same source. I don't think that I wanted to express a certain thing and then develop the music around it, it was just me moving in a new direction and everything I did changed... I had just decided – not even decided, it was kind of involuntary – that my passion for country had subsided. **1992**

I have to clean house once in a while. I have to totally switch directions and even philosophies. I went through a... total metamorphosis. This album is very introspective. Very from the inside. **1992**

It was very painful this time, but also a great release, a real catharsis. I wrote based on totally personal experience and feelings. Having to operate on my emotions was very difficult. It was a challenge to broaden myself while at the same time to become more introspective. I had to become more vulnerable, more naïve towards a song, toward myself as a singer, to be unafraid to show the softer side of myself, to just be as honest as possible. **1992**

(*Ingénue*) was about something I had to forget, all right, but that doesn't make the forgetting any easier. **1992**

Ingénue's aspect of falling in love was more about the elimination of the guard I had on myself. It doesn't really have to do with the other person, but to do with how love affected me this time. Also, in getting older I became more vulnerable and more honest. By losing control I mean a deeper sense of vulnerability, of being at the whim of God. Accepting yourself. **1992**

Obsession is a weird thing, like an unhealthy sort of exercise. *Ingénue* was this great work of art, this great gift, this great gesture: you see, I'm really in love with you, look what I've done. Now that it's basically over, it's sort of going: No, it's yours Kathryn, it's yours. You wrote it, you sang it, it's your record, not hers. **1993**

It's not really over. It's just that it's kind of an unattainable love. It's just a feeling for somebody that I can't have right now. I was more than a year into it when I started writing the songs. But it's basically about the process of being in love, and it's really about me. It's not really even about the other person. **1992**

It means the other person's married. **1992**

This was the easiest and the hardest record I've ever made. Tracking was a dream come true. The hardest thing in the world was to get those vocals. When I started to do the vocals, I was singing from the writer's perspective. If you had the choice, do you really want to sit there and cry for a couple of hours? **1992**

I think what happened is my earliest influences surfaced, like classical piano, being the youngest of four kids who all studied classical piano. Film music, soundtracks and Broadway stuff were also early listening influences. I think having the passion subside for country allowed those influences to come to the forefront in a strong way. **1992**

The evolution of singing the songs live helps. Different memories become associated with them and they become different things. Certain shit comes seeping in once in a while. The emotions are there and they come from a very natural place, a sort of unconscious state. **1992**

I thought I'd lost it, I thought my voice was taken away from me. I practised for hours, while walking through Paris, Berlin, Stockholm and Zurich. I discovered that I'd been singing from the wrong place. When I came home, I got it. **1992**

You take all these pieces until you actually start writing or actually finish the record. I couldn't mould it into any genre. **1992**

We still have all those beautiful sounds, accordion and stand-up bass and real vibes. It's a really beautiful organic mix. We're mixing about half and half from the back catalogue with this new record (*Ingénue*), and it's turning into this real neat trip. We have some delightful exotic surprises, reworkings of old stuff. And it's about singing this year, as opposed to getting the crowd up and dancing around and being very kinetic. I'd never want to have to repeat myself. It is a different show. I can warn people and entice people with that. **1992**

At the very beginning of rehearsals, it looked like it might be hard, but then we worked hard on new arrangements of the old stuff and very hard on the sequencing of the show. I thought at the beginning of the tour that singing the country stuff was going to bore me, but it's quite the contrary. When I get to the part in the show and I'm doing the old stuff it's like having a beer with a close friend. The show is basically one cohesive, exotic trip. It's a lot more introspective and womb-like than my old shoe, but it is cohesive. I pour myself into it all. **1992**

Ben Mink on *Ingénue*:
The fact is that in our eight years of collaboration we have only got together four times to write her entire body of work. It comes out very quickly, *Ingénue* was written in a week and a half, though we agonized for ages over the arrangements, and she over the lyrics. We sit down with a couple of acoustic guitars and talk, but we'd start off a song with anything. If the kitchen clock falls to the ground and clanks in a certain key, that can give us enough of an idea to start something. The song *Miss Chatelaine* was written in about 15 minutes. **1992**

There's not really a place for the type of singer I am. So, I think it's really about creating your own space through your influences. Ben Mink and I really tried to allow the music to lead us, to be very naïve and innocent with it and let it surface through us. **1992**

I definitely suffered from opinion anxiety in the beginning. But fortunately, my musical collaborator Ben Mink and I have been working together for a long time. We knew we were in a whole new area, and we were very careful. **1992**

It was wonderful. In fact, Ben would take two wildly different artists – say Kurt Weill and Buddy Merrill – record them on two different channels, and mix them together. So we'd be listening to a Hawaiian steel guitar over Kurt Weill. It was great. **1992**

When I talk about unfulfilled desire, it's not just human physical love. It's the love I feel for animals; it's the love I feel for trees. **1992**

You know, the video (*Constant Craving*) is loosely based on *Waiting for Godot*. **1992**

I'm talking about constantly craving this person I'm in love with, but I'm also talking about why I feel I need another person.
You know, I've never seen a blue heron with another blue heron, have you? You know blue herons? They're always alone. But they must mate. **1992**

(*Miss Chatelaine*) was completely my concept. I wanted to expose
the Lawrence Welk induced part of my personality. I would actually
like to explore that side more, because I think I've been kind of
guarded, and my masculine side has been more able to proceed
in society than my feminine side. But now I am feeling more
comfortable with it. **1992**

I never really considered (*Mind of Love*) a song. I considered that
a conversation with God. I wrote it in this very room, on that little
typewriter that my friend bought on the street in New York for $10.
1992

I think the songs are the kind that are malleable to me. They can
reflect either melancholic or, hopefully, romantic emotions.
Those are recurring feelings that we all go through. And sometimes
you feel more in control of a situation and sometimes you don't.
1992

Ingénue isn't a pure form of anything. People always say,
"Well, she doesn't have her own style." But thank God, I hope
I never stop changing and searching. **1992**

salmonberries

(I play) a half-breed Eskimo tomboy. It's a story of a relationship
between these two women. It borders on a love story but it never
really consummates. **1992**

I would have explored their relationship more... But in their
aborted lovemaking scene, I think it was a very real way of dealing
with it, because I think that's exactly how the librarian would have
reacted. I know that one of the first times I ever had someone
come onto me, I sort of went, "No." Then, "Well..."

I love acting. It's not my first love, but it's sure something I'd like to
have an affair with. Because I am a big media figure. That's part of
the game. There are moments when I'm high on it, moments when
I think it's garbage. **1992**

I'm sure I'm going to get a lot of gay roles at the beginning, but
I'm more interested to expand. **1992**

I'm actually interested in doing a really straight feminine character.
1992

stage

When I was 5, I competed in a couple of local festivals, like a Kiwanis type of thing...Well, they would have somebody come down and judge. I sang a song called *Robin In The Rain* and I won. I'd sing at showers and weddings: *Midnight Blue*, *Silver Threads And Golden Needles*, *The First Time Ever I Saw Your Face*. Everybody knew what my dream was, but nobody ever said anything. The only thing my mum ever said was, "If you're going to be onstage, you're going to need braces." And I'm glad I got them, because I feel so much more confident now. **1992**

Being onstage is my element. It provides the gravity to the whole thing, so, in that respect, I love it. **1989**

I totally dig the stage. It's the same feeling I had when I walked into a gymnasium and could smell the sweat: its potential. I feel the space and feel the potential. I feel a strong connection to God when I'm onstage. Art is my way of communicating love. **1993**

When I'm onstage, it's the most comfortable place on earth. I love to sing, I *loooove* to sing. **1993**

The best part is looking out into the audience and seeing all the different kinds of people who make an effort to come to my show: old couples, gay guys, teenagers, young 14-year-old boys and girls, yuppies – the whole demographic. There's new people and old fans both, which makes a real mix of people who don't know anything about you and who know everything about you. **1992**

I can't see the real logistics of it. I can't see the audience, and I don't go out into the lobby. When I am leaving the show, it's always women backstage waiting for me to come outside. That's obvious. But my sound people and my manager tell me that the audience is everybody. There are families, and I get a lot of fan letters from older women, 60 and up. **1992**

For me, it's singing in front of an audience. There's a commitment, and it would be cheating if I didn't give everything I had. **1990**

What I do onstage is completely natural – it's just the way I react to my music. I'm very energetic; but I'm worried that people will think I'm cow-punk.

My ears can only take so much. I like to do the sound check and the performance and sleep. Then we go to the next town. **1992**

I don't have a private life on the road. I do have a home and a lover and a dog. It's difficult because you have to incorporate that when you go out, but then when you go home you have to sever this part. **1990**

I put so much out into my show that I don't do anything creative during the day. I do interviews and try to find food and ride the bus and that's about it. **1990**

the reclines

Well, they're friends and family. And we love what we do. That's why we spend hours on the stinky old bus. **1990**

What's worked for me and what I like doing on stage is changing from a man to a woman in terms of physical appearance. There is a little bit of shock, like the wind cleaning out cobwebs. **1988**

It's important on stage because both men and women are attracted to me. I think there's a locked-up tomboy in all women and I think there's a locked-up more feminine side in all men. **1988**

If it's an Elvis song, I replay an Elvis character. I think being almost a chameleon is a good quality. **1988**

I try to look at everything in all dimensions. I try to deliver a song like *Johnny Get Angry* with layers, so that a member of the audience who has been abused can go, "wow, she's talking to me," or a guy who's sitting there dreaming about slapping his wife can also feel something from it. I received a letter the other day from a feminist saying, "I'm really upset by you doing *Johnny Get Angry* because I can't figure out whether you're condemning or condoning it." I would assume that a woman who looks and acts like me, well, it would be pretty obvious what I felt about it. But you know, that's fans. That's the way people are. **1990**

That's what I thought singing was about. I didn't think I did it fraudulently, it was just a matter of not knowing. My record-making and performance happened simultaneously, so country music for me was very much about projecting, about being the entertainer. I always thought I had to ascend into character. But with *Ingénue* I went completely the opposite way; I really pulled on the strength of subtlety and internalizing, searching for passion inwardly. **1992**

The stage gives you the emancipation to do things. Because you know there's always been cross-dressing onstage – always, since theatre began. And it's the place to do it. It's about art transcending sex. But still retaining sexual elements. **1992**

I don't make political statements on stage every night. **1990**

Calgary (Olympics)... That was another scary situation. My heart was jumping out of my body. It was a big responsibility – not only representing my country, Canada, but also playing for 60,000 people in the stands, and then right before I went on, they told me that there were something like 2 billion people watching worldwide. I said, "Thanks, I really needed to know that." **1992**

the UK:
In Glasgow it was almost like a Lawrence Welk show. And I love that too. I think the lesbian factor has a lot to do with the film (*Salmonberries*). I find that I like the energy of women in a concert. But they can be the most overbearing and disturbing fans, because they feel like they have a connection with you: "You're a sister. Gimme something!" **1992**

fame

being a star

I've always known that that's what I was, that was what I was going to be. It's not even like an immodest thing. It's like somebody saying 'I'm going to be a doctor.' It's not a big deal. I've known since as long as I can remember. **1993**

I was imagining travel. I was imagining being onstage. I was imagining lovers. I was imagining owning something like a place like this. I imagined what it would be like when I was older. **1993**

It's my reality. It's tiring, but that's all relative. Working eight hours a day is tiring. I guess the biggest sacrifice is just giving up your right to anonymity. Maybe that's just a matter of growing older.
1992

I'm a living example of success via the media. I've never had radio airplay, I'm a media thing. **1988**

It's like people think you have more choices when you're famous, but actually it really limits you. It's more limiting than ever. **1993**

Joni Mitchell's the only person with whom I've ever been star-struck. **1992**

Success has alleviated a lot of judgmental pressure. There's no question. **1992**

My mom keeps it in perspective; she makes sure I'm not getting too high-headed. I'm not self-righteous enough to think I'm unique and I'm not over being rebellious, but I've learned that to just go your own way and be yourself, which is what I'm trying to do, is alternative to a lot of people. **1988**

Success robs you of your anonymity. And that robs you of your spontaneity. To me that is sacrificial. **1988**

I think I would also like to go somewhere like Zimbabwe where no one would know who I am and sort of conjure up some spontaneity again. **1989**

It's very difficult to change when you are working so hard, and once you establish celebrity or some public image, you're always sort of on the defensive. I'd like to be anonymous again. **1989**

Artists are put in a trap. They attain success, and there's pressure to do it again, so they just basically write the same record again. It's very hard to stay away from such formulation where there's so much pressure to make the money while you're hot. **1993**

I'm not interested in producing for success. I don't think I'm ever going to be selling 42 million records. My legend isn't going to be based on sales, but hopefully on longevity and the purity of the product – one being unique and doing it my way. **1993**

I'm not at all in a hurry to become famous. I like to work hard, I like the challenge of touring and the challenge of the business. But I'm not in a hurry. One of my goals is to keep dissatisfied. I am very conscious of not checking out and just going through the motions. It's like really bad sex. You're not reciprocating the gift, and you're going to feel really awful. The pressure I feel most is the pressure of being an artist and of having to create. No one's making you do that. That is a gift – or a punishment. **1993**

I die when people criticize me. I totally fall apart. **1992**

It's a very small-town mentality, to criticize and hate when someone has done well. I was talking to Joni Mitchell who also experienced rejection by the Canadian people after success; she said in Canada they eat their young. And I'm told in Britain they do the same thing. America doesn't suffer from that, for some reason. **1990**

I don't understand why people have the need to turn on someone who's successful. I know I do that with hockey players and other artists. But it doesn't feel good when you are the recipient. **1990**

God... what is normal? Is it normal to work in McDonald's? Is it normal to be a star? **1989**

I'm the kind of person who tends to blurt out what I shouldn't blurt out. **1992**

To be a star, to me, was saying I want to sing, I want to be an artist. There were points in my life when being on the cover of *Q* magazine or *Vogue* was an exciting prospect. It still is, but now the goals have slightly shifted. I've achieved some of my material goals – I've bought a small farm which was always a big dream of mine – and when you've achieved those peripheral goals of what you're doing, you have to analyze and understand what your aspirations really are. **1990**

No one hands you a text on how to become and remain a celebrity. But because I've been doing it for 10 years, I just don't know anything else. It is my life and you learn to adjust. **1990**

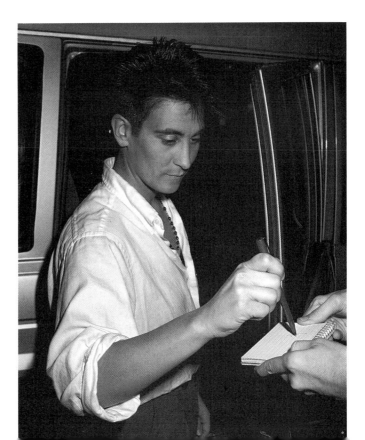

One of the benefits of the way my career has developed is that it's been gradual. Each time I've achieved a new level of success, I've had time to readjust and observe. I am k.d. lang and that's the bottom line. **1990**

I feel like I can be myself more than ever and I'm not defensive about it. (Fame brings) this unconscious pressure that you're constantly being observed and judged, that your energy is wanted. At the same time if you go for a certain period when you're not recognized, this animal inside you goes, 'What's happening?' **1989**

private life

Private life is when you get into the hotel room after gigs and interviews. It's about three hours a week. **1988**

I get itchy if I'm in one place too long. I don't really feel like I'm ever home anywhere.

My life may seem complicated to someone unfamiliar with the business, but I do keep things simple compared to the way some entertainers live. Once or twice a year I dress up and do something glamorous, but generally, I don't like night life. I'd rather stay home and cook and then go for a walk. **1992**

The public wants to know dirt about celebrities for the same reason people enjoy seeing fights and hockey games – it's displaced aggression, and because of that I used to find doing interviews an ungodly experience. I don't feel that way any more, and I've become less guarded with the press, but I still believe my private life belongs to me. **1992**

There's things I don't want the public to know because they're special, just like if you slept with someone you wouldn't call your mother up and go, Hey, I just boinked somebody. There are things you want to covet, to cherish, for yourself. That's a human instinct, not because I'm a star. **1990**

Though it influences my art, I don't talk about my personal life, because the art is foremost. Some famous photographer once said, 'To suggest is to create; to describe is to destroy.' You can apply that to my personal life and my art. **1992**

I used to see a separation between my public and private life, but I think that was just the youth of my understanding celebritism. **1990**

I guess I just have a boring existence. People are doing biographies, but there's nothing interesting about me. I don't think they should do them until you're dead. You just do something because it feels right. I mean you can analyze it to death, but... **1993**

k.d. with Liza Minelli and Chrissie Hynde.

sexual identity

women

I really pride myself on being 100 percent woman, but with this great luxury of pulling from both sides equally. **1993**

I think there is a definite alliance between women, because we're an oppressed people. **1990**

I think women have a different spirituality than men. We share the same emotions basically, but social structures always have been set up by men. Almost always. Even Tampax is made by men. **1992**

Let's go to the anatomy here, the basic difference in orgasms: Men's seem to be very local, very about "out" – you know. Women are very internal, very all-encompassing. A woman's is more oriented toward birth and about the cycle. It's two different – real different functions. Which is great. I mean, obviously, it's the way of nature. **1992**

I'm offering women something that they don't have a lot of: a strong example, something that's geared more to women's feelings. But no one ever says "Why, at football games, is it 90% men?" It's another example of why women are constantly scrutinized about having some sort of bond. I mean who cares if they're lesbians? **1992**

I am a feminist. I don't care if the women I reach are lesbians or not. I don't even care if men come. Music transcends. But women have to realize that we're different, and we have to find some way of making that difference known inside ourselves. **1992**

Maybe by just being good at what we do, and being strong, and not being manipulated by men. My personal fight against (sexism) is not to fall into social formularization of what a woman should be. Although I don't necessarily hate an image like Dolly Parton's, because that's how she feels comfortable. I'm saying... individuality in women is important. There's a strength there. **1990**

Why aren't there more women (in music)? There's this thing about having babies. Do careers and babies match? I personally don't think so, but that's just my point of view. Because music is my lover and my child. **1992**

I'm a strong and self-assertive woman. Women generally like to follow artists like that, because there are not a lot of examples in our society. Maybe women find solace in what I'm saying. **1992**

If you want to know the truth, I am so much a woman. I am as womanly as I could be. With my lovers, I am completely a woman. My body is completely a woman's body. When you get to know me, I'm a total woman. I think the male thing is just a way of surviving – outside. Inside I'm completely a woman. **1992**

androgyny

I think it was a vehicle for people to say I was gay without having to ask me the question. **1992**

I like to look androgynous because I don't like to use clothes as a sexual tool, and my career has benefited from the fact I've bucked gender stereotyping. **1990**

I'm androgynous, (it's) synonymous with k.d. lang, a polite way of having people speculate. Country music is very old-school, male-dominated, Christian-oriented. It's probably everything I'm not on a lot of different levels. **1992**

(Androgyny) is definitely not for shock value in my case. It's more about accepting myself; it's how I feel most comfortable. Like my hair: I wear it short because I think I look better with short hair; it's not a political thing. **1992**

In fact, it's difficult for me to explain, because it's really natural. It's this sort of balance between things I'm attracted to and the kind of clothes I feel comfortable in. I wouldn't look good in a little red dress, anyway. So it's really just incorporating your looks with what you feel comfortable with. **1992**

I look goony in long hair. I do! I have this strong jaw that's really nice onstage, and if I have hair that's long, it covers up what I think are my best features, my sharpness. And I end up looking very plain. Do you want to know a more practical reason for having short hair? When I'm onstage I sweat and my hair goes flat, and it looks really awful. **1992**

First, I don't wear makeup – if we're going to do those makeover shots, "before" and "after", I'd show me "after" as being much prettier without makeup. I'm a very androgynous looking woman, and my goals are not to be a wife or necessarily a mother. Androgyny is important in my life because I can deal with people on a human, not a sexual, level; it's important on stage, because both men and women are attracted to me. They were to Elvis Presley too. It's important not to eliminate possibilities for people. **1988**

It's just my natural response to how I fit into society – how I feel comfortable, how I feel confident. If I had to wear high heels and a dress, I would be a mental case. **1992**

k.d. with Sandra Bernhardt.

I'm not very comfortable with (my body). My body is very womanly;
I think that's why. Or maybe because it's so overused in the
entertainment industry. Maybe it's a deep rebellion. I don't
understand my own feminine power yet, in terms of my body.
I don't know how to use femininity as a powerful tool. I use my
sexuality, but I eliminate gender from it. I hesitate to use the word
"androgynous," because it's overused and misunderstood, but
androgyny to me is making your sexuality available, through your
art, to everyone. Like Elvis, like Mick Jagger, like Annie Lennox or
Marlene Dietrich – using the power of both male and female.
1993

I like to pretend I'm a farmer and sort of dress for chores.
Always ready to feed the cows, drive the tractor, fix the truck.
1990

The boys can be attracted to me, the girls can be attracted to me,
your mother... your uncle, sure. It doesn't really matter to me.

I want to intrigue people, to play with them. I love paradoxes.
Any contradiction excites me. I like to be cryptic.

I'm trying very hard to project a strength that goes beyond gender.
A good singer is like a good painting. A good painting attracts
everybody. It isn't limited to one group. I don't want to attract just
men or women. I want to get empathy from everyone while I'm
singing. **1990**

I'm not afraid of being called androgynous, because I'm not the
typical female role model even though I am 110 percent woman.
I would like to be dealt with on a human rather than a sexual level.
1989

People want to know why I'm androgynous, they want to know if I'm gay – they want to know. I'm different. I mean, I don't think I'm that different. I get a little tired of the issue, because ultimately I'm a musician. **1992**

coming out

I am what I am... I don't want it to be a big deal. I don't because I agree with you totally – there is a point where you just go, "OK, enough"... because I know how the people are. I know how the press is. **1992**

There's been a lot of speculation in the press. So I think I'll just come out right here and now. Yes I am a Llllll... opez fan.

I came out (to my mother) 13 years ago... And I think my mother's proud of me for being an individual and being brave enough to talk about it. **1992**

k.d. came out when she was just a young teenager, so it wasn't like some hideous trashy lesbian pulp novel from the '50s. She wasn't, like, tortured about it. **Keltie Lang, k.d.'s sister. 1993**

I was having problems with my girlfriend, and my mother said, "What's wrong?" I said, "You wouldn't understand." She said, "Try me." I didn't want to lead a life of dishonesty with my mother. I wanted her to understand me. And had known this for years and years and years. **1993**

I go, "Mum, if they ask me, I'm gonna not lie to them." She lives in a town of 650 people... and I've tried to move her out of there. **1992**

But it's hard, because I mean she's lived there 30 years, and that's where her friends are. **1992**

And that's gonna hurt our relationship. And that's why I've always hesitated to be really, really out. I'm still worried about this article... I know the repercussions are gonna be there. It's like, I want to be out. I want to be out! Man, if I didn't worry about my mother, I'd be the biggest parader in the world. **1992**

I think everyone knows. The people who like me, like me for my music. And that's the way I want to keep it. I have to say something else. I don't want to say the wrong things to the gay culture. Because there are so many different opinions on how to

k.d. with Flotilla De Barge, at New York's
Hard Rock Café, February 1993.

gain acceptance and how to just live normal lives. And we're
fighting amongst ourselves, I struggle too with all the answers and
the questions. And I don't want to hurt my mother by coming out
in the press. But at the same time I don't want to hurt my culture,
and it's like – what do you do? **1992**

I am not responsible because she is another human being,
and she is living her life to learn as well. But the beef controversy
hurt my mom quite a bit, I think. And it freaked me out about
controversy. I would probably be a lot stronger otherwise.
Maybe I'm stronger now. I don't know. But the thing is, after I
started to regain my composure and my confidence about being a
public image, and I started going, "OK." I talked to my sister about
it, and then doing this film (*Salmonberries*), you think the gay issue
is gonna come up. And you go, "OK, what am I gonna do here?"
I don't want to lie. I'm not a liar. I try not to be. And yet you go,
"Is your job as an artist more important than the love between
a mother and a daughter? Or is lying to 'protect' your mother the
biggest sin of all?" It's an ongoing question. **1992**

It's basically a choice I made, and to have the issue over with.
It's always been an undercurrent, the question of androgyny.
I'm a little tired of it and I want people to focus on my music rather
than to some day have to be defensive about it to the *National
Enquirer* or something.

When I'm asked the question I say yes. But I don't want to sit
here and talk about it, although we are. It's the nature. Because
it's just like if I spent my whole conversation with you talking about
my vegetarianism. I try to deal with my sexuality in a humorous
way, because that's how I feel comfortable. Let's talk about Freddie
Mercury for a minute. There's a really amazing example of
someone who called himself gay as a daffodil. He sold a lot of
records and sold them to people who usually are gay bashers.
1992

The age 28 to 31 has been a big period of re-evaluation and
refocusing. It's more of a feeling, an intuition, than a redefining
of a philosophy. The freedom of coming out, of having switched
genres and having success has really relaxed me. I feel more
secure and confident in trusting my instincts. **1992**

I wanted to be responsible to the community, and in 1992
we're struggling for acceptance. I also wanted to be responsible
to myself and not have to act defensively because of some tabloid
atrocity. And I felt that it was probably better, in the long run,

that I just be honest and open about it rather than be someone who is always speculated about. **1992**

I don't feel political about my preference. I just don't. I'm sorry! I'm sorry to disappoint you hard-cores, but I don't! I think as a human being we all feel discrimination at some time; we all feel oppression. There should be strong examples in the subculture, and I think there should be people fighting for our rights. But I don't feel like it's my passion. I feel like it's a part of my life, my sexuality, but it's not – it certainly isn't my cause. But I also have never denied it. I don't try to hide like some people in the industry do. **1992**

I don't think I sacrificed anything (by coming out), but I didn't know that at the time. My career could have been over. In the industry, they thought that could happen to me. So I was freaked. I agonized over it. My biggest fear was my mum. When I did it, I called her and we had a cry. Any mother wants to protect her children and see them be happy, and I think she thought people would be more negative than they were. **1993**

It was totally positive, totally positive. Like an emotional veil had been taken away. The really, really big thing I experienced this year was the intimacy between me and the audience, not just because of the number of women, although that's part of it. It's that I feel comfortable knowing that they came there knowing. That I don't have to worry that if they finally figured it out, they would get up and leave. (That fear) is there in a lot of gay performers. And being out is just great. I recommend it to people who are ready to do it. Just do it. **1993**

I think it's important for people to come out, because it's broadening the acceptability walls. But I always thought I was out. I presented myself as myself. I didn't try to dispel lesbian rumours. I sang songs like *Bopslina*, which was about my girlfriend. I didn't take boyfriends to the Grammys. I didn't do anything to cover it up; I just lived my life. There was a part of me that really didn't think it was important to make an announcement. But to the gay community saying "I'm a lesbian" is dispelling any doubt. **1993**

sexuality

I'm not black, but I might as well be. I'm white, Canadian, and *erm*, questionably something... questionably whatever.

I think there's a deep pool of pain, a deep hurt that I manifest in different ways in my life. That is not why I'm gay; it has nothing to do with that. But there's a difficulty trusting, and it's exacerbated by being famous. I think resolving it, and understanding how it's affected me, is something very deep and intricate, and I'll be dealing with it all my life. **1993**

When I was five, I remember playing Batman and Robin. There was one point in the play where we were going home to our spouses. I was playing with two little boys, and they said they were going home to their wives. I said I was going home to my wife too. They said, "You can't have a wife!" I said, "Yes, I can." I remember that really clearly. My earliest memories are of being attracted to women. **1993**

I think (being gay) is a lot of things. I don't think it's any one thing. I think it's a choice, for some people. I think it's genetics. I think it's the result of being abused, like a reaction. I think it's completely natural in some cases. I don't know why I'm gay. I find women more enticing, both emotionally and sexually. **1993**

I think sexuality is something that you should use. It is a part of life. But I'm careful about it, because I don't want to alienate anybody, gay or straight. My goal has always been to have a very diverse audience. **1992**

(Culture is) always in a mess. I don't think that will ever change; I think it will shift. We're not that old as living beings, so I'm not surprised that it's so slow. As a gay woman I would love to see homophobia dissipated. We've come a long way, but the pendulum will constantly swing back and forth. **1992**

I was just thinking about this particular interview and how lately my lesbianism, because it is itself a closeted issue, becomes the focus, and I have to be the Lesbian Authority. Although I want to talk about it, like I want to talk about my vegetarianism, I'm a singer. That's what I am foremost. With the lesbian-chic stuff, I feel like I'm being used as a representation when I didn't come out for any other reason than to alleviate a lot of personal pressure. **1993**

I'm approached quite often by gay institutions to be a spokeswoman, but to me coming out and being a strong example of an artist is as strong as I can get. I want to be known as a professional artist and not as a professional lesbian. My sexuality is part of my life and I no longer have a problem talking about it, but I don't want to be known strictly as a lesbian. My music should transcend that. **1992**

Lesbians have been the rudest to me on the road. They think I owe them something. They want me to go out to a club with them, but I don't like clubs, gay or straight. I've been to lesbian and gay conferences. I've worn a pink triangle. Where did it get me? I admire gay activists, but I'm an artist.

I'm certainly not ashamed of my orientation, but I also don't want to be a spokesperson for gay and lesbian rights. At least politically. Through example, perhaps, and through my music, maybe, but I don't want to be labelled a lesbian singer. That's not my goal, because it's just one aspect of me. **1992**

on the rumours k.d. was dating martina navratilova:
That was really the epitome of how ridiculous it all is. It's like all celebrity lesbians must date each other. It's kind of an insult. Not because of Martina, who's awesome and who I really do like and love as a friend. **1993**

I have been called "sir" so many times in my life and will always be. **1992**

lovers

I would hope I can attract both men and women. And that when a person is attracted to me, they're not thinking about my genitals. **1992**

teenage lovers:
Anyone I could get my hands on, basically. **1993**

All the women I ever saw ended up marrying somebody from one of their classes and staying in Consort and having kids. And I thought, "Oh my god! There's got to be other ways." And so whenever an intelligent strong woman came to town who looked independent and who had gone to study at a university and had travelled around, it was like, "I want to get to know you." **1992**

I was definitely a stalker. **1993**

Although I don't like being the initiator all the time. **1992**

Women send me their 8-by-10s and their measurements, but the last thing I want to do is sleep with a fan. Because k.d. lang the performer is so much cooler than me. Not that there's really a difference, but as a lover I'm not as self-assured and cocky and invincible as she is. **1993**

I think I sabotage relationships because I'm afraid of being left again. I'm extremely loyal, but I'm extremely scared, so I just do things to tamper with things so I can get rid of it so I don't have to worry about it leaving... Maybe my potential true love is reading this and saying, "Oh, she's never going to be able to have a relationship!"

I think the ultimate lover will be like being alone. It will be so comfortable, I won't have a problem sleeping or feel I have to entertain them or worry about them understanding me. I think I'll know her when I see her. I hope. My biggest insecurity is my body, being big, I have a big complex... I do have a big love. **1993**

qualities in a lover that k.d. likes:
I'm sort of a pantheist, so that would help. And they would
probably have to be a vegetarian or wanting to be. I guess it's
basically a narcissism. They have to be kind of similar in beliefs
and life-style to me. Not in looks, though. I'm attracted to really
diverse people. And I like people who are different than I am...but
I'm kind of attracted to mutual narcissism too. The dirty side of
me is. **1992**

They have to have some assimilation of belief, as I do. **1992**

k.d. with Liza Minelli.

I like nice bodies... No, actually – I want to retract that. I really do. Let me retract that... I want to replace it with somebody who is healthy... meaning someone who has respect for their temple. Who tries to take care of themselves. **1992**

I like seeing two boys together who are on the same trip. **1992**

I have a little bit of penis envy. Yeah, they're ridiculous, but they're cool. As much as I hate it, I admire the male sexual drive because it's so primal and animalistic. I think that's one of the reasons women have a hard time with them, but it's one of their greatest assets; there's a certain freedom in that. It's very elemental. **1993**

I think female sexuality gets convoluted because of social pressures. All these different ways women are pulled – everything from being a virgin to not being a virgin, getting pregnant, having a nice body – I definitely have been affected by that disease. **1993**

I was watching MTV and there was this young girl group – I can't remember their name. They have a song called *Not Too Proud To Beg* or something. These three girls – they're probably 16 or something – and they're talking like, "Come on baby, let's go fuck." And I'm thinking, "You know you're just a kid, just starting to have sexual feelings, and everyone's telling you, 'Don't have sex.'" That must be really a trip. And yet I think in some ways, you know, the question of reconsidering promiscuity is a good thing. I mean, it's been good for me to sort of go, "Well do you really want to sleep with a lot of people?" I mean it's good for your ego, but is it really? I think sex is a good thing, and I think sex is an important thing, but it's not the thing.

You know, I've never actually gone through therapy, so I don't really understand how this all works. I'm sure it's because my father left the family when I was 12, and my teenage years were with my mother and I think probably the fact that I'm a musician and I love to travel and that I'm constantly alone in a hotel room has something to do with it. I think sometimes that I'll never be granted a lover, because I've got one. It's my voice. I don't know if that's a really pathetic romantic artistic thing to say. **1992**

Singing is the ultimate. It's a very emotional thing, very emotional to turn yourself inside out and ride each nuance and each note. It's what I live for. I was asked, if I had to give up lovers or music, which would I do, and I said I would give up lovers. Music is the ultimate to me. I think I would easily give up the music business before a lover, but not the actual singing. **1990**

future

I am quite happy with what I have accomplished. I couldn't have asked for more. **1988**

I plan to put in a few good years of hard work and retire early. **1988**

What I would like is to be respected as a singer. But who knows? I'm on the verge of buying a small farm on an island off Vancouver. **1990**

I've got a lot of dreams, and they don't all revolve around music. I'd like to be a farmer. I'd like to be an actress, a painter, a motorcycle mechanic. I dream every night that I play for the (Edmonton) Oilers. **1988**

I'm sort of interested in doing *Annie Get Your Gun*. **1990**

What I would really like to do is take a little sabbatical to allow myself to change a bit. I'd like to get back together with a few friends and do some performance art or some gallery shows. **1989**

They're always saying I'm almost there. Almost where I'm supposed to be. I'm always on the verge of something. And that's just where I like to be. It's once you get over the edge that you have all the trouble. **1992**

I think I've been really honest and open about the fact that I'm
not married to any one genre and I've changed in the past and
I may change again...It's what comes out of my soul. I could do
Ingénue again but I don't know I will. **1992**

There's a part of me that wants to be middle-of-the-road, and a
lot of people shudder at that. I was thinking about calling my
music "alternative easy-listening." In trying to appeal to everyone,
"middle-of-the-road" is what fascinates me the most. I don't really
like to offend people...see middle-of-the-road to me is the safest
and the unsafest place to be, because you're that much farther
away from the ditch but you're that much closer to being hit by
oncoming traffic. What intrigues me is being alternative and being
completely conformist at the same time. And that's actually
how I try to live my life. **1992**

My goal now is to stay creative and have a career of longevity
and history. I want to feed the muses, to sustain the reciprocity

between me and what makes me an artist. I intend to stay an artist of integrity with brave force, to stay moving in a straight line at a direct pace. It boils down to that. **1992**

Foremost, I want to stay creative. I want to keep the reciprocity between the muse and my actual product. Feeding what feeds me, keeping the creative taps running – that's always scary.

As you get older, especially in the music business, you concern yourself with being on the edge. But I think my edge will be in my singing. I think that for as long as music inspires me, I will have no idea of what I'm going to become. My palette just keeps getting bigger and more complex. It's quite possible I could put out a heavy-metal record when I'm forty-five. **1992**

I would like to be global instead of local. As everything – as an artist, a spiritualist, a cook, a singer. It doesn't feel like I am. I feel like I'm known and recognized and listened to, but I always feel like there are these major mountains I have to climb creatively. **1993**

I'm changing all the time. Someone remarked to me just the other day: "Champions adjust." So anything could happen. I could meet a Tibetan monk and shave my head bald. **1993**

I always feel like I'm just beginning. **1993**

what others say

You look like a boy, dress like a girl, and sing like a bird.
Roy Acuff, perennial Grand Ole Opry host after k.d.'s performance

We admire k.d. for her voice and because there is nothing phony about her. I'm tied to this costume, this persona. Not k.d., she's not tied to anything. I think k.d. represents the freedom we all wish we had. I love her. She has such a pure, beautiful voice. I hope it doesn't vitiate.
Minne Pearl

I think the lady has a complex. We play what the audience wants to hear, and we play her. But she's got to face the fact that if she is going to be the Boy George of the country music scene, she's going to get some snippy comments.
Larry Nelson, country radio station owner (WAUR-AM)

Elvis is alive – and she's beautiful.
Madonna

My God, she's a female version of Sean Penn. I could fall in love with her.
Madonna

You don't look for a copy, you look for an original. I think we found one in k.d.
Owen Bradley

There's so many things that can happen to people who rise so fast. I have nightmares about it.
Audrey Lang, k.d.'s mother

k.d.'s Top Desert Island Albums:
The Patsy Cline Story – Patsy Cline
Hard Hitting Songs for Hard Hit People – Hazel Dickens
Season of Glass – Yoko Ono
Country Hits, Vol. 7 – (K-Tel)
Latin A La Lee – Peggy Lee
"A Kate Bush album, although I'm not sure which one."
Wild, Wild Young Women – Various Artists (Rounder)
Gerald and Oscar Peterson – (Pablo)
Rickie Lee Jones – Rickie Lee Jones (Warner Bros.)